When He Leads.... I Will Follow

The road to a successful marriage

Owen E. Ford, Jr. & Julia D. Ford

When He Leads... I Will Follow
Copyright © June 2016
By: Owen E. Ford, Jr. & Julia D. Ford

Published in the United States of America by
ChosenButterflyPublishing LLC

www.cb-publishing.com

Editor: Stephanie Montgomery, Unique Communications
Concepts
Photographer: Shooterz Photos
Cover Layout: Artful Kingdom

All rights reserved under International Copyright Law. Contents and/or cover may not be reproduced, distributed, or transmitted in any form or by any means or stored in a database or retrieval system, without the prior written consent of the publisher and/or author.

ISBN: 978-1-945377-99-0
First Edition Printing
Printed In the United States of America
June 2016

You can contact the authors at: **truelovechurch@hotmail.com**

Table Of Contents

Foreword	5
Opening Thoughts	7
Ch. 1: The King Discovered	9
Ch 2: I'm Putting Away my Childish Things....	13
Ch 3: Obtaining Favor as a Husband	17
Ch 4: I've Got Nothing but Love	21
Ch 5: Can I Give my Husband a Little	23
Ch 6: No One Ever Taught Me How	29
Ch 7: There is Power in My Yes	35
Ch 8: The Queen Revealed	41
Closing Thoughts	45
A Prayer for the Wife	47
A Prayer for the Husband	49
A Prayer for Both	51

Foreword

Owen E. Ford Jr. and Julia D. Ford are awesome and a power couple. Like the name of their ministry, they exemplify 'True Love'. We respect, love and appreciate them enormously. They are a very patient and loving couple, who wear humility gracefully. They are a powerful couple who walk in oneness and complete everything with a spirit of excellence.

Husbands and wives are to submit to God and to each other. Husbands are to love their wives as Christ loved the church and gave Himself for it. Wives are admonished to submit yourself to your own husband. (Ephesians 5:22-24). Wives are to respect her husband (Ephesians 5:33).

In this book "When He Leads I Will Follow" Owen Ford Jr. and Julia Ford, take you on the road to a successful marriage by giving insight on how a husband should lead his wife and family. Wives will be encouraged through biblical principles, Godley advice and words of wisdom, to respect and honor the husband. Wives will learn how to be followers of her husband and respect him as king in the home. Husband will learn to love the wife, be a leader in the home and community without fear. On this road to a successful marriage, you will fall in love again, building each other up and walking together in agreement.

We have been married for 26 years and it is a journey which is continuously evolving. Marriage is instituted by God and intended to be forever. As you continue on the road to success within your marriage: "When He Leads I will Follow" will be just the book you'll want for your marriage journey. It will remind you that God+ You + Your Spouse = SUCCESS.

We know this book will bless you tremendously.

Richard and Nephetina L. Serrano
Co-Founders,
Covenant Marriages, Inc.
Life Coach, Biblical Counselors,
Author and Visionaries
"Together Forever, We Are One"
www.covenantmarriagesinc.org

Opening Thoughts

Soon-to-be-married couples are encouraged to get pre-marital counseling. Once they are married, what happens next? Some couples are in need of a little more help after they say, "I do". Through the trials and tests of marriage, couples may discover they need a refresher course on how to keep the marriage strong. This book will aid those who seek the road to success for their marriage. You will learn to examine your marital character and then make adjustments where needed. You will be encouraged to find your own marital paths, while embracing the journey walk together.

God has intended for the husband to successfully lead his wife and family. God also intended for the wife to follow her husband's lead. Many people, things and mindsets can cause this not to take place. It's the enemy's job to separate what God has joined together. It is the will of our Father in Heaven to ensure that your marriage prospers and is in good health. Let us help you make this happen.

Husband; it is our sincere prayer that you will lead your queen and family with confidence, compassion and love. Wives; it is our genuine desire that you follow your husband's leadership with faith, trust and a renewed mind.

We declare this to be so in Jesus' Name, Amen.

Chapter 1

The King Discovered
On the road to leadership

Husbands, it is important to become comfortable as a leader to your wife and children. Leading our wives and families is our God-given responsibility. Leadership is the action of leading a group; a community, a family, or an individual. Leadership requires attention to detail; the ability to problem-solve and excellent communication skills, amongst other important attributes. One of the most important things we must remember as husbands is to not run away in times of adversity; you must lead through adversity in order to bring your wife to the place called peace. You should not leave decisions solely up to her during such vital times in your marriage. She needs you to lead; she wants you to lead and when you lead, she will follow.

The issues which can plague a marriage are plenty, but the solutions to the majority of them stem from your leadership. If you are a husband who is not assertive and soft-spoken, that's ok. You can still lead her. At times, a strong woman may not believe you are assertive enough to match her emotions when a problem arises and as a result - she may have the tendency to make decisions without you and inform you later. If you are a husband who is assertive and controlling, you may be leading with an iron hand. Leading without emotion or compassion is not good leadership.

Control and manipulation rob your wife of the ability to see the heart of her husband leading her as God would lead and love her. This is when you must discover the King in you. Be the king of your castle, be dominate and mark your territory. In addition; be the king of communication, reconciliation, support, strategy and finance. Most importantly, be the king who loves and leads your wife to the throne room of God our King.

When a husband says he has a problem leading his wife, in my opinion - that says he has a problem loving his wife as well. Through my years of counseling, I have observed wives talk to their husbands disrespectfully and act out of line. This is not acceptable behavior for the wife to display, I might add. This type of behavior will only put the husband on defense against the wife, instead of allowing him to be 'on offense' against the adversary.

What I have learned, is that if you lead your wife by loving her - it will lead her to respect you. Through counseling, I discovered a majority of the wives were disrespectful because they didn't feel loved by their husband. In a marriage - if there is no clear headship, a power struggle ensues. Husband, if you are not leading your wife then who on earth should or would she follow? Your wife must be led with love and attention to her details. She must be understood and shown the way she can be appreciated without losing her identity as a wife and mother. Your wife needs you to lead, wants you to lead and when the king (which is you) calls, she will follow.

There are many great examples of how husbands lead their wives - such as salsa dancing. The husband must lead his wife or partner in the dance and she must follow his direction. He decides the next move and she flows in his rhythm. She accents the moves by adding her feminine twist and flow. They are in sync and compliment one another's movements. This is an example of great leadership and it starts with the man.

Chapter 2

I'm Putting Away My Childish Things....
Maturing in my leadership

When you get married, it is time to put away all of the childish behavior and mindsets you developed when you were single; childish behaviors like selfishness, jealousy, the 'blame game' and having tantrums when unable to get your way. Behaviors as such, are 'ticking time bombs' in our marriage and are immature. These types of behaviors can lead to a toxic marriage. One of the most deadly and toxic behaviors to bring into a relationship, is selfishness. Marriage is not all about you or your way - nor is it 'reward only' without sacrifice. Husband, you cannot primarily concern yourself with just your needs and interests in a marriage. You must consider your wife and value her interests as well. This can be difficult to achieve if the husband and wife are unable to agree on what direction the family should take.

Selfish behavior varies, here's one example: The husband wishes to take an exotic trip and leave his wife and children behind in order to have 'alone time'. This is dangerous because this behavior may allow for another woman to enter into what is declared as only 'your time'. The devil will attempt to have the lady in the blue dress fill your time and cause you to lose priority and focus. You're 'alone time' still belongs to someone else.

This is not a mature way to lead your wife, husbands. The male ego will suggest that she can have her 'alone time' and you can have your time alone as well. This is a gross error in leadership. This self-centered behavior is injected into the marriage at a high cost. The result will be the husband requesting a divorce or separation if the wife (the weaker vessel) falls prey to the enemy's tactics during her 'alone time'. We must review how this mindset entered the marriage. It was allowed to enter through the selfishness of the leader of the marriage, which happens to be the husband.

Marriage calls for a mature leader who is able to put away his childish things so that his wife doesn't become a 'fall guy' for his bad leadership. The maturation process takes time as you grow and learn your wife; however, you should always strive to be at the high end of that process - not pilfering at the low end of immaturity.

A good husband grows as he goes; filling his own shoes which were once too big. A good husband follows a biblical outline and has mentors to help him mature and raise the level of excellence in his life. A good husband bands the house and doesn't seek the opportunity to tear it apart. A good husband loves his wife and appreciates the task to lead her. A good husband must have good morals and not use his upbringing as an excuse for poor leadership. A good husband is one who encourages and supports the success of his wife. Jealousy is never an option. A good husband will realize that immaturity is the enemy to your happiness in marriage and it will prevent you from being the husband God wants you to be. A good husband is one who is accountable and accepts the responsibility of the husband; the father and the priest of his family. When he leads, she will follow.

Chapter 3

Obtaining Favor as a Husband
Seeing my wife as a person of value, not my possession

In life we place value on our homes, cars, clothing, food, etc. These are all possessions that we own. You cannot place value on a human being and in this day and time, neither can you own a person - however, the person in your life can be valuable to you. Your wife must be a valuable person in your life and you should honor her as such. Anyone would give you more of themselves if they see that you appreciated what they bring to the table. Husband, you must be careful not to look at your wife as a possession. This can be dangerous. Understanding that your wife belongs to you and you only - is not a declaration of ownership. Marriage is the joining together of two people and they become one flesh, according to the bible. The man is the head of the wife as Christ is the head of the Church.

We should lead our wives with Love and Grace like Christ leads and loves the church. Viewing your wife as your possession will lead to control and manipulation. Control means to dominate; to command by way of possession. In a controlling marriage, abuse can become prevalent. Verbal, emotional, mental and physical abuse are all tools of control by way of possession. This is an unhealthy and toxic way to establish your role as a leader. Many women suffer from this type of treatment and it is not acceptable by any standard.

Leading by control will lead you both beyond boundaries you never thought you would cross. No one has all of the right answers or the best ideas for the marriage, so consider what your spouse has to say. When I started to value my wife, she began to produce beyond expectation. She gives me her all every day in our marriage. My advice to you husband, is that you do the same. Stop looking at everything she does as being wrong. Find a reason to compliment her and give her reason to take ownership in the marriage. Show her that she adds value to you by investing in her. Make her secure, rather than engaging in criticism sessions. When you show your wife that you value her, your respect level will go through the roof.

The Value of Love

Love does not have a price tag attached. You have to love unconditionally, even if you receive negative feedback. Show your wife that you value her. Make the expression of love a constant in your home and promote unity. It's good to learn her love language and speak it often. You will receive eye contact which says 'you get me and if you get me then you must love me'. Lastly, love your wife enough to consider her opinion. Even though the decision is yours to make, don't make it without her input. She will stand by you in the good and the bad, because you show that you value what she brings to the marriage rather than treat her like your possession. When you lead, she will follow.

Chapter 4

I've Got Nothing but Love for You Baby
When I learn to love her genuinely... we both win

Some husbands have difficulty loving their wives the way they should be loved. When there is no true love, the ability to lead becomes compromised. This could be due to personality conflicts; differences in upbringing, misunderstandings in the marriage or disrespect from either side. These may be valid issues, but you must come together in agreement with your wife about the love you share for each other. Determine what keeps you together and build on that. Difficult times will occur in a marriage - but you must unite and create a fortified front. When you learn to love your wife genuinely, you both win. You win against all odds of separation and divorce. You win against the forces trying to destroy your marriage and cause you to abandon your promise and responsibility.

When you learn to genuinely love your wife, your children win. They win because they see and know that forgiveness and reconciliation are what allows their parents' marriage to work. Loving your wife brings the word of God to life in your marriage. Husband, your marriage can be an example to others who may be where you once were. You can teach the next husband how to genuinely love his wife through thick and thin, ups and downs and through good and bad.

Now that you've discovered the king in you and value your wife - you can establish the marital relationship which is the foundation of everything you and your wife build together. When you love your wife, you will not compromise her safety, her security or stability. You will also lead her the way she desires; she will be happy because the love of her life is leading her and will not have difficulty following.

Chapter 5

Can I Give My Husband a Little R.e.s.p.e.c.t?
Respect is a word of love

The Bible says in Ephesians 5:33 NIV; *"However, each one of you also must love his wife as he loves himself, and the wife must RESPECT her husband."*

What is this word called RESPECT? The Merriam-Webster dictionary defines respect as a feeling of deep admiration for someone. It is very easy to deeply admire someone when they are giving us what we want or need, or if they are doing us a favor. It takes no effort on our part to cheerfully say, "Thank you" to someone for their multiple acts of kindness toward us. Respect is a two-way street. We should give and get respect. The lives we live should cause a person to have deep admiration for us. Some feel however, that if they are not getting respect, then they will demand it. The demands will come through verbal threats and or physical mistreatment. Beloved, this ought not to be so - especially if we proclaim to be saved by the shed blood of Jesus Christ.

Somewhere throughout our lives, disrespect has become more prevalent in our marriages than respecting one another. We have learned how to be mean, nasty, hateful and destructive with our words and actions as women - even more so as married women.
It has become very easy to partake in gossip, slander and 'throw shade' on other women, which makes it easier to do the same to our husbands. We have become very comfortable cussing, fussing and demeaning our husbands as Christian women. We have made disrespect the new normal in our lives and homes. What kind of foundation have we as Christian women, laid for our daughters for when they get married? Are we encouraging them to consider an alternative relationship, lifestyle or being single because of what we - as married women, have displayed through our examples of disrespect? Will our sons - through their married mother's negative behavior, attitude and verbiage towards their fathers, grow up believing this is appropriate treatment?

Our husband's pride and manhood should never be stripped down by our hands. Why is this acceptable? Why is it ok to freely disrespect our husbands behind closed doors or even worse, out in public? Who gave the free lessons on 'How to verbally beat down your husband 101'? Who encouraged you to sign up for the next rotation of classes called, 'Hit 'em in the face and kick 'em below the belt 102'?

Beloved, if you find that you have been a willing participant in these acts and others like them - please stop. You are doing yourself, your husband, your children and your marriage a great disservice. You heard the saying, "Do unto others as you would have them do unto you." Your Father in Heaven doesn't disrespect you. He loves you with a great love. Why, oh why sister would you feel comfortable with treating your king, your protector and your lover with disrespect? Many of us do not feel the need to show respect or admiration to our husbands because we are broken from our childhoods or are offended, hurt, insulted and filled with the inability to forgive people - including our husbands. You feel as if you owe your husband for all the pain, shame and neglect which he and others caused throughout your life and marriage.

The Bible says to owe no one anything except love. It also says that "...Vengeance is mine said the Lord, I will repay". Owing and vengeance are not in your hands to execute, but guess what my sister? According to the Bible, you will reap what you have sown. Sow a hard heart, you shall reap pains in your heart. Sow joy and happiness and reap an easy fun-filled life.

As Christian women who are wives, we strive every moment to bless the name of the Lord. We make sure we go hard in worship and praise. Every chance we get, we quote a scripture to let God know we are getting His word. How many of you know it's out of alignment with the word of God to love Him whom you have never seen - but to hate the brother or sister you see every day? Simply put; how can you love and tune-in to God and you have never laid eyes on Him – yet at the same time, you cannot admire the man you called husband at the altar on your wedding day? Beloved sister, I encourage you to first repent to God for harboring such ill feelings towards your husband. Repent for not forgiving him honestly and totally. Next, forgive yourself. Release your heart so you can begin the healing process needed to rebuild you and your marriage. I declare that the marital pains tormenting you shall never rise again. I speak that your heart shall beat regular beats per minute once again.

Due to hurt, pain, shame - even guilt throughout your marriage; you have shut down emotionally from your husband, disrespect him and undermine his authority. Lastly, some of us carry non-matching marital baggage due to the way we met our husband and how or why we even got married. Unless there was a gun to your head, you willingly stood at the altar or justice of the peace as his wife. Marriage isn't easy, but it sure is a good thing. When our marriages are flowing with respect and love, it's very sweet and nothing can compare. In fact, the Bible says that when your husband found you - he found his good thing and he obtained the favor of the Lord.

No matter what you think, feel, speak or even look like; you are his good thing. Don't allow anything or anyone to convince you otherwise. The Bible says that he receives the favor of the Lord because of you. What is a favor? Favor is defined as acceptance, good will and delight. Because of you sister, God looks upon your husband with acceptance and delight. Truth be told, as our coverings - we need and should want the Lord to do this on behalf of our husbands. Our husband's lives will run a lot smoother when the Lord is looking upon him with acceptance. When our husband's day and life are running well, then so will ours. This will allow you to admire the beauty of God shining through his life. Could your lack of respect for him as your husband, your provider, your friend - be a partial root cause of the marital pains you are experiencing?

Sister, by no means am I trying to convince you that every marital woe you encounter is solely your fault. What I would like you to do is take a deep look at yourself, your behavior, actions and mouth to determine ownership for your part in the dysfunction of your marriage. Our husbands have a responsibility to help heal our marriage, just as we do. Both husband and wife must be willing to rectify the marriage.

What does respect look, feel and sound like? It looks like peace has finally arrived in our homes. Not a place without flaws or wrinkles; but a home filled with talking, laughter and intentional listening to one another. It feels like an atmosphere that is balanced. It doesn't have a stench of competition, envy or jealousy. Respect sounds like the best jazz band on a warm summer evening. When we openly show admiration, praise and delight in our husband - we will experience a new found level of joy within our marriage.

Giving and showing respect to our husbands doesn't mean we will have trouble-free days, it just means there will be fewer days of sorrow. Let's make a commitment to follow our husband's leading. Wife, you are now empowered to follow.

Chapter 6

No One Ever Taught Me How....
How to overcome the not knowing

Wives, it is very easy to duplicate what you have seen someone do. It requires no effort to mirror another person's actions, whether right or wrong. Truth be told; how many of us were taught how to obtain and maintain a healthy marriage? Who served as your example of marriage? What did their example teach you? Did it make you want to duplicate what they showed, or did you rebel from the very thought of marriage based on what you saw or heard? Confession is good for our soul. Acknowledging that you don't know how to obtain a healthy marriage - let alone how to maintain one, is the first step in your recovery. In fact, it is maturity and shows you are willing to humble yourself. Allowing yourself to accept the fact you have not been a great helpmate called 'wife' is not a dead-end road, it is just the opposite; it's the beginning of your 'come up' in your God-ordained marriage.

This chapter will help you realize some of the marriage faults you created or continued. Once you can identify your participation in the breakdown of your marriage, it is then time to restore it the right way - God's way. Depending on your upbringing, you either viewed marriage as an abundance of joy, or an insurmountable amount of pain. If you have a great marriage free of frustration, miscommunication and stress - then this chapter is not for you. Bless God for what you have; kiss and hug your king, then go and teach another sister what it takes to make it work.

However - if you have or are experiencing deficits in your marriage, such as; lack of communication, lack of support and lack of love - then this chapter will encourage you how to get your marriage back on track. The enemy to our success as married women is the lack of knowledge. If you don't know how, when or why it's necessary to speak to your husband kindly and with respect - then you will always shoot from your emotions and end up tearing down the very one you are charged to build up. If you don't know when, how or why it's important for you to build your house through proper management, then it is evident your home is in constant disarray - and more probable than not, so is your marriage. If you don't know why you should never withhold sex from your husband, or use it as a punishment or reward system - then you could possibly add cracks in your marriage which allow the enemy to enter through unclean spirits.

My sister, saying "I don't know" or that "No one ever taught me" is ok for a quick moment; however, that should not be our final resting place. Our marriages require daily work. Sometimes in order for a thing to stand firm within the sands of time - it must be tested, tried or proven. If it is to stand on sure footing - cracks, holes and splits in the foundation must be located. If you find your marriage in this situation; don't give up, don't give in and for goodness sake - don't fade to black. Have reassurance that some of the most beautiful statues have brutal, weather-beaten marks. Monuments have endured restoration processes and some of the most amazing wonders of the world withstood serious neglect of maintenance from their builders. Understand that many weapons formed to break down and break up your marriage, however through the grace of God - they just could not succeed. Know that your Father in Heaven is committed to seeing you through your marriage restoration - and guess what my sister, He will never leave what He created.

Your marriage will be a masterpiece; it will come through the fire refined and retuned. Some may view your marriage as another wonder of the world. This is a great place to shout Amen to the hope our Father desires for you to possess. He will see you through and the spirit called 'I don't know' will cease to exist as the third wheel in your marriage.

Let's start by forgiving all the people whom you believe should have told you, who should have taught you and who should have warned you. Go on, I will wait a moment.

After a while, your declarations of not knowing what to do or how to act in your marriage will become an excuse. How many of you realize that excuses don't explain and explanations don't excuse? Eventually, we as wives must grow up. We must face what we committed to and pledged our love towards. Stating that you don't know what it requires to get your marriage back on track is an easy and simple way to prevent taking responsibility for your part. Our goal is to be open and honest about what we did or said which caused disruption to your husband, children, household and even you. Today, tell yourself you will no longer make excuses regarding why you cannot have a healthy marriage. Make a pledge to honor and recommit to those vows you declared to the world what may seem like a lifetime ago. Look in the mirror and tell yourself you are finally breaking up with all the excuses that sowed discord, mistrust and pain in your marriage.

Next, let's review a few possible reasons for our lack of knowledge concerning how to improve of our marriages:

Fear of Doing the Wrong Thing

Some of us grew up in very critical homes and environments. For a great portion of our lives; we were instructed what to do, how to do it and when to do it. If things were not completed to the satisfaction of the individual - then we were scolded, chastened or corrected.

This type of upbringing may prevent an individual from trying something new because of the possibility of failing to meet another's approval. Hurting someone's feelings or not living up to their standards may hinder a person from thriving to their fullest potential. This fear of failure and disappointment can transfer into your adult and married life. My dearest sister, you must find strength within yourself to break this yoke of bondage. This fear should no longer grip your life. The fear of failure can be so intense; you may find yourselves experiencing panic attacks, nightmares and feelings of anxiousness. The bible says that God has not given us the spirit of fear - He has given us love, power and a sound mind. Well, sister - it's time to 'get up off that thing and dance 'til you feel better'. It's time to serve your divorce decree to the enemy of your marriage and tell him you are no longer a willing participant in his game of, 'I DON'T KNOW HOW'. It's that simple beloved; fall out of agreement with the enemy's plans for your life, your marriage and your ability to make things work.

Not Wanting to Know

There are some wives who really don't want to know how to have a healthy marriage. There are wives who could care less about putting forth the needed effort to correct their marital wrongs or strengthening what is right. As a child of God, first and foremost - you owe God, yourself and your husband a valiant effort to try and fix, adjust, correct or enhance the marriage you made a vow to God on your wedding day. The spirit of laziness is not profitable for your marriage. My sister, clear your vision and remove the cobwebs from your heart and eyes. You must find worth in your marriage. You must find a reason to fight against the enemy, instead of fighting your husband. It's the enemy's job to separate the both of you. Not only does he hate unity; he really hates unity that is anointed. All the enemy desires is a small crack in your marriage so that he can easily enter.

A wife that is too lazy to exert the effort needed to repair her marriage is exactly 'the crack' the enemy seeks so that he can devour her, the husband and ultimately the marriage. Sister, do the work and prevent the enemy from winning over your marriage. You and your husband are worth it. Push yourself to go beyond what you saw, heard and felt growing up. Your marriage doesn't have to end the way your examples in life ended. Tell yourself the curse of separation and divorce stops with you. Tell yourself you will find the energy needed to get back on track.

My dear sister, not knowing how to overcome marital obstacles and challenges is not the way out of your marriage; it is just the beginning of discovering what it takes to make it better.

God + You + Your husband = SUCCESS. A corrected mindset will enable you to follow your husband's leading.

Chapter 7

There Is Power In My Yes

Finally, I'm surrendering to my husband's leading

Sing: I surrender all, I surrender all,
All to thee my HUSBAND
Whom the Lord has given to me
I surrender all

Take a deep breath... now exhale. I may be one of the few people who'll tell you it's finally ok to surrender to your husband. Not only is it ok to surrender to your husband; it's ok to finally give him the room he needs to lead you as his wife. Surrender is defined in Webster's dictionary as the following – 'to give in; to give way; to submit; to cave in and to back down'. Most women find it challenging to give in, give way or even submit to their husbands because they were not taught to do so - or their perception of surrendering is unclear. As women, we mirror what we see other women do. Who were your examples? Are you mirroring Clare Huxtable from the 'Cosby Show', or Rosanne Barr from the show 'Roseanne'? Are your marital characteristics more like June Cleaver from 'Leave it to Beaver' or Peg Bundy from 'Married with Children'? Now, after considering whom you resemble most - how is it working for you?

Are you delighted with your efforts in surrendering to your husband's leading of you and your family - or are you unable to surrender to his leadership for different reasons, therefore you've decided to lead yourself? If the latter is your lot - my sister, you are on a slippery road as a Christian married woman. The bible tells us in Ephesians 5:22; "Wives, submit yourselves to your own husbands, as unto the Lord." This word 'submit' means to consider another's advice. Are you in a place to consider advice from your husband - or do you know everything? Are you broken from past hurts, failures or from something which has nothing to do with your husband?

Do you find it difficult to submit to his voice, his direction or leadership? Beloved, there comes a time when we as wives must finally put away our childish antics, tantrums and vengeance towards our husbands. We must come to the realization that he is designed to lead us and our family. His leadership skills and qualities may not currently be at 100%, however if we encourage and support his efforts to lead - then he will strive toward growth.

We cannot teach our husbands to lead, however we can let them know what works and what doesn't in our families.

There may be reasons unknown to you regarding why his leadership skills are not up to par. What examples did he have in front of him growing up? Were the examples positive or negative - or did he not have examples throughout his life concerning how to lead a wife and family? Just as we may not have received good examples of how to be a submissive wife that honors her husband and builds her home; he too may not have had the best examples to show him how to properly love his wife and raise his children strong. As long as the both of you have a willing heart to get your marriage back on track, the enemy cannot win. My sister, you can start the ball rolling. You need to adjust your attitude concerning your husband's leadership - then have a conversation with him discussing your marital goals and family dreams.

It's very easy to discuss things he did or aren't doing which don't qualify him as a leader in yours or anyone else's lives. How about this; since you already know the details of what he did or did not do, for the sake of arguing who's right and who's wrong - let's say that you wife, are right. He doesn't deserve to be a leader or even called one. But guess what - you wife, stood at the altar and said "I do". When you said "I do" that meant you co-signed everything he was then and would be in the future - and the same for him concerning you. He also co-signed to all the days you chose not to cook or clean. He too said "I do" to the days you didn't feel like following his leadership, therefore no one can claim they are a victim in the marriage. Both of you have a responsibility to make the marriage work. Both are equally responsible for exerting the needed effort to honor God through your marriage. Wife, his dominant role in your marriage is to lead you into your destiny and purpose. If you clear your eyes; there is a God-given vision on the inside of your husband for your life that doesn't include you being his slave or his puppet. Instead of seeing and agreeing to what's inside of him - for you as his wife, the enemy wants division to occur which leaves you both distracted and off course for your lives.

Wives, our husbands are given by God the task to set structure in our homes and it's our task to honor that structure by keeping it in order. Often times we find ourselves doing both; but there are some wives who do neither of the two. We must finally reach a place of saying yes to setting the order in our marriage and in our homes. Nothing good comes from chaos and confusion. If the structure or order is out of place, then where does that leave our children? What are they seeing? What are they learning? What will they eventually duplicate when they get married?

My sister, once you finally say yes to your husband's leading - you will experience marital power. What kind of power? The power to overcome many obstacles and challenges together; the power to declare a thing together and it shall come to pass. We must get to a place of agreement with our husbands. Not agreeing to disagree - but agreeing to agree. By no means am I asking you to agree with something that is not of God - as that would be harmful to you, your family and marriage. Please be spirit-led while considering what your husband is asking for in agreement. After hearing what your husband says concerning setting the structure for your home and lives - use your 'yes vote' and agree.

Do not withhold your 'yes' because you wanted to set the plan, you didn't like the plan or you want to be spiteful. Your 'yes' woman of God - is a sweet sound in his ear. A wise woman builds her home and her 'yes' is a brick laid in the foundation.

Decide today that you will follow your husband purely and freely. His leading is only good if you are following. If you don't follow, then your husband is simply taking a long, unproductive walk. So wife, unfold your arms; stop pouting, rolling your eyes and get to following. If you still are not willing to follow his lead because of his character flaws etc. - then pray for him. Pray your husband to be what God has called him to be before he married you. Pray for his mindset, his character, his attitude and his strength. Pray he makes God number one in his life. Pray that he takes his leadership of you and your family seriously. While you are praying for his development into the king he is destined to be, do not become uncooperative. You can't pray and hate at the same time. You can't pray for change in him, yet you are staying hard-hearted and unforgiving. Prayer will soften your heart if it is true prayer. Make sure you involve God in your marriage, instead of informing him what He must do to change your husband.

My sister, it's my prayer that you follow your husband with smooth and continual strides - not stutter steps.

Chapter 8

The Queen Revealed
Happy to be in stride again

Sister, prayerfully through these few chapters you have started working towards you and your husband being in sync again. Some may have found these chapters to be a tough pill to swallow. Some may feel this book is just a maintenance check for their marriage. Either way, I am sure we can agree there is always room for self and marital improvement. Every now and then, we need to check the temperature gauge in our marriage. Are we arguing more than usual? Have we become more involved with others outside of our home, rather than spending time with our husband? Have we lost the excitement to see one another? Are we no longer physically or spiritually intimate? If you said yes to any or all of these questions - then you wife, you must do something about it. Stop worrying that he will not receive what you are doing. If you are genuinely praying for you, your husband and your marriage; if you are truly changing yourself without looking for a pat on the back - I promise he will see your pure efforts and the change will take place. Many of us did not get into our marital jams overnight - therefore, we should not assume we can eliminate them overnight. Returning to what you once had may be a longer process for some, than it will be for others. As long as the process is 'going', then bless God. As long as there is life in your marriage, then bless God. Don't give up on you and your husband. Do not hand your marriage over to the enemy. He desires to receive it; don't do it sister. Give it one more try and find safe, Godly counsel. Let this book help reignite your commitment to your marriage. Let it be the aid you need to change your ways, your mindset and attitude towards yourself and your husband. It is my true prayer that soon and very soon, you will be singing:

"...I'm just happy to see you and me
Back in stride again
Woohoo woohoo..."

With our head bobbing and fingers snapping; I tell you wife, you are able to follow. You are equipped to not only follow your husband's lead - but to do so with a smile on your face. You do not have to imitate the destructive paths of other marriages. The buck really can stop with you. You can begin again and your marriage can and will be successful. God meant what He said in His word that what He has joined together - no man, woman, boy or girl can tear apart. Check the three-fold cord holding your marriage together. Make sure God is the third person in your marriage and you will never go wrong. Behold, old things have finally passed away and behold, all things have become new. Do not allow yourself to keep a record of wrong-doing. Keep your heart and mind free and clear of yesterday's past. Look forward to tomorrow. God is there and so is your husband.

My sister, I speak life into you so that you may follow your husband and teach other women to do the same. I declare that the dark cloud over your marriage is finally removed. The sunshine has arrived and the dawning of a new day is here. Bless God for your life and another chance to honor your marriage. Now run to your husband, your king and tell him you love and respect him. Make sure he knows that you are recommitting yourself to honoring the vows you spoke to each other on your wedding day. Now give him a kiss and a hug, and then make plans to go on a date.

Closing Thoughts

A Plan Worth Working

Zig Ziglar said, "If you fail to plan then you plan to fail". Beloved, you and your spouse MUST plan to succeed in your marriage. Your marriage will not be successful simply because you said it would. Your marriage will only be as successful as the committed work and dedication you BOTH put forth. Marriage is a marathon - not a sprint race. It requires equal participation from both the husband and wife on a regular basis. It requires consistent, positive reinforcement. Take time to listen, laugh and enjoy one another. Don't get so deep into your life that you forget each other is a part of it. It's ok to go the extra mile to make each other smile. A call, text or a card in the mail can go a long way towards letting each other know that you are thinking of them.

Don't stop holding hands. Intimate touching is priceless. Do not wait until you're in the bedroom to become intimate. Intimacy begins in the car, kitchen, living room, etc. Take a quick moment throughout your day and kiss each other - then resume your daily routine. Learn to fight the devil together instead of each other. He is the real enemy in your marriage, not your spouse. He becomes defeated every time you both recognize he is 'throwing shade' and is 'hating on you'. It's not your friends or family; it's the devil from hell that wants your marriage to fail.

He is the one sending the singing telegrams from hell called 'marriage breakers' to your home, heart and mind. Quickly return them back to the sender by praying, fasting and studying God's word together. Agree that your marriage is not next in line for divorce.

I believe in you and your spouse. I know for a fact that all things are possible to those who believe. Having a healthy marriage is possible. You actually loving one another is possible. You growing old and happy together are possible, if you just believe.

A Prayer for the Wife:

Father in the Name of Jesus, I ask that you meet my sister at her point of need. I ask that you enter into her heart, mind and soul. Father, I come asking for forgiveness of our sins. Father, I ask that you strengthen my sister. Give her the grace and wisdom to honor her marriage vows. Give her the peace to follow her husband without losing who she is in you. Let her know that it is ok to begin again. Please remove all shame, guilt and past failures and hurts. Renew her mind in you and refresh her spirit. Father, thank you for loving my sister unconditionally. You have made many ways of escape for her time and time again. God, I ask that you bless her with Godly strategies on how to build her home. I rebuke the demonic spirits which are trying to invade her thoughts and actions that will cause her to react negatively toward her husband and family. Father, allow my sister to know that you created her with a great purpose in mind. You desire the best for her. Please let my sister know that she is fearfully and wonderfully made. Father, I ask for the scales upon her eyes to be removed in Jesus' Name. I speak she will be healed, delivered and set free to love again.

In Jesus' Precious Name, Amen.

A Prayer for the Husband:

Father, in the Name of Jesus, I pray that the husband reading this prayer finds peace and comfort in this prayer. I pray that he will be the standard-bearer in his home, the protector of his wife, the leader of his family and the man you have called him to be. I also pray for the spirit of encouragement to come upon him. I ask that you lead, guide and direct him in your holy wisdom. In Jesus' Name, I pray that the husband will finally find value in his wife. I pray for the power of agreement to be evident in his marriage. This new found power will cause them to experience great marital success. I also pray that this husband will know that you are his provider and only through your grace and mercy, can he provide for his family.
In Jesus' Name, Amen.

A Prayer for you both:

Father, in the Name of Jesus, we thank and praise you for this couple. This anointed duo in the natural and in the spirit. Father, we ask that you heal their marriage. Heal the ties which are binding them together. We speak that the marriage-breaking spirit will not win. We declare that every demonic assignment against their marriage shall not come to pass. I speak that the fiery trials which have come to destroy them shall be returned back to the sender. I release ministering angels to soothe every rough edge in their emotions, morals and intellect. Father, don't allow the devourer to come and snatch their finances or means to get wealth. Allow them to see more prosperous days together.
In Jesus' Name, Amen.

www.ingramcontent.com/pod-product-compliance
Lightning Source LLC
Chambersburg PA
CBHW061302040426
42444CB00010B/2475